To Mike & Jill
from
Jill & Tad x

Frankly Speaking

Excerpts from the True Memoirs of a Remarkable Cat:

Frank E. Forsythe

dictated to and scribed by

Annie Forsythe

Published by Annie Forsythe,
C/- P.O. Box 61,
Peregian Beach, Qld. 4573, Australia

Telephone: (07) 5448 1277
Email: perecon@bigpond.com.au

Second Printing 2001

ISBN 0-646-39324-3

Designed and Typeset by Bracewell Typesetting

Concept and Production through Joshua Books,
P.O. Box 5149, Maroochydore B.C., Qld. 4558
Phone: 0413 757 547

Joshua Books

Drawings
by
Jim Somers

Dedication

This book
is dedicated to
Cats, Catophiles and Adventurous Spirits
the world over.
May the sun always shine
on your whiskers
and Curiosity guide your pawprints
into the Great Unknown.

Frank E.

Contents

Scribe's Note

Every story in Frank's Memoirs is true. Frank's Consulting Veterinarian, 'Charlie' who lives and practises on Queensland's Sunshine Coast, can corroborate most of them.

All the characters, both human and animal, are real; only the names (with the exception of Frank, Ernestine, Jessie and Maddie) have been changed.

Since Frank cannot type, I have undertaken to do it for him but as these are *his* memoirs, I feel obliged to report faithfully the world as he sees it. Therefore, there are occasions when characteristics (such as Henry being 'thick') reflect Frank's opinion rather than my own.

Annie Forsythe

Vet's Note

"Dear Frank,

I'm just writing to say thank you so much for your 'honest' appraisal of your visits to my abode. It's always good to get 'actual' feedback from your *real* patients – rather than the human clients, that is!

Yours sincerely,

Charlie

'Charlie' The Vet"

Acknowledgements

(by Frank E.)

I would like to thank my Number One Frankophile, Dick, who wrestled with the great heap of technical stuff involved in producing this book. I did try to help but Dick insisted on doing all the computer work himself. So I just wandered across the keyboard from time to time, pressed the ***'delete'*** key and sat on him for company.

Thanks to Annie for the secretarial services, to Jim for the beaut drawings and to 'Charlie', 'Rose' and Carol for keeping me alive to tell these tales. Thanks also to all my mates who encouraged my writing and gave me such great feedback: Em, Lovely Jan, Lionel, Christina, Cally and John B.

I could go on and on with this thanks business but it gets boring after a while. And anyway, the book's about me, so let's *. . . read on!*

Introduction

'Cat's Whispers'

Allow me to introduce myself. My name is Frank E. Forsythe, I am not quite five years old and I've had a very interesting life.

I live on the Sunshine Coast at the top of a hill overlooking the ocean. I own the hill and a pole house which I share with two quite decent humans, Dick and Annie. The hill became mine when I inherited it from the original owner, Mike, who went to live in Catheaven. Maintaining ownership has been difficult at times and every so often I am required to remind various would-be usurpers (other cats, dogs, snakes, rats and humans) of my authority. But I share my hill with my friends and before I expose the pages of my memoirs to your sniffing, inquisitive gaze, I would like to introduce you to a few.

Across the road lives a lady named Emily. Em fancies me, I know. Even when Mike was living with her, I could tell Em fancied me. Em lets me inside to carry out Daily Inspection. If I'm tired she lets me have a little nap on her bed.

Over the hill lives Henry. Henry's me mate. The only trouble with Henry is that he gets over-excited and when that happens he tends to get a bit rough so then I have to slow him down with a quick little nip. Then he gawps at me through his glasses and says, "Aw, jeez, mate! Whadjerdo that for?" Then he laughs and we start playing again and I have to try to remember to be gentle with him. He can't help it; he's a bit thick.

Henry lives with Sid, another good-looking Burmese gentleman like myself. In the mornings (after I've been to Em's) I go through Sid's cat-door for Daily Inspection of their house and if Sid or that damn fool Sausage Dog have left any food, I clean it up for them. Then I go and see whether Henry's still in bed. If he is, I wake him up. If he's not around I might have a bit of a nap there myself.

Down from Henry lives Jill. Jill is wet about cats and has two moggies, Ben and Bruce. Ben's a gentleman, but I can't say the same for Bruce. Bruce is always challenging my ownership of the hill. Jill is quite happy for me to carry out Daily Inspection and even says I can lie on her bed if I want – but not Bruce. Bruce needs sorting so it's up to me to do it. More on that later.

Down the road is Lionel. Lionel used to live with Wendy but she went to Catheaven too. Lionel doesn't always make his house available for Daily Inspection but he does have a very nice sunlounge in a delightful little courtyard which I may use any time I please.

Next door is a cat named Tammy. Tammy's nice but very shy. We get on fine because she does everything I tell her to. Tammy shares her house with Judy and Brian and a wonderful toddler called Buzz, who thinks I'm the ants pants, and a pet rat named Barry. I tell you, I'd like to play with that rat but they won't let me near it. Judy and Brian fully understand the necessity for Daily Inspection and are no trouble at all. Actually, they are pretty cool humans, I'll tell you why later.

Apart from that, my most 'significant other' as the wanky phrase goes, is Charlie. Charlie is my Consulting Veterinarian. Charlie has good reason to be extremely grateful for my patronage: money. I keep him in money as you shall presently appreciate.

These are the central figures in my life. Others come and go. Nearly everyone loves me because, you see, I'm a very lovable cat.

Dear Reader, the following excerpts from my memoirs will enable you to get a glimpse of my life which, I can assure you, is anything but dull. I hope you will enjoy them.

Yours sincerely,

Frank E. Forsythe, Esq.

'The Cage' 1

I shall begin my tale at my tail end. I was born the second son of a litter of five Burmese kittens. My mother, while elegant, was sour-tempered but my dad was a wonderful, easy-going chap from whom I inherited my excellent character and humour. My conception was a contrived event orchestrated by a couple of 'breeders'. (The 'breeders' are really my mother and father but you can't tell humans anything; they think they know it all.)

I was born with a broken tail, right down at the base, so that if you view me in full frontal – or full arsenal for that matter – my lovely tail goes straight into the air about one-and-a-half inches off to one side of my body. It is quite distinctive.

Right from the moment I hit planet earth I felt destined for a life of adventure. In fact I was so gung-ho that except for my father's cautionary advice, I'd have leaped straight into the arms of the first humans who wanted me. *Don't be hasty in the selection of your human minders, Son,* said Dad. *Decide what sort of qualities you want them to have. Do you want a Sooky-Protective type, or a Worker-Mouser? Do you want a Pets-for-Kids type or a Show-off who values looks and breeding above character? Do you want an Indulgent who lets you get away with murder or an I-Just-Want-To-Be-Able-To-Say-I've-Got-A-Cat type? Do you want* ***them*** *to run* ***your*** *life or do* ***you*** *want to run* ***theirs****? These are important considerations, Son; so be sure to choose very carefully.*

It was good advice and as soon as he said it, I knew straight away which sort I wanted: ***Indulgent***. And I was determined to wait for the ***most*** indulgent I could find. To this end, I tried to avoid 'The Inspection' in case anyone should discover what a wonderful kitten I was. 'The Inspection', by the way, is a very undignified selection process carried out at an age when one is too young to defend oneself. Hoisted into the air, tail held up, bum peered at, privates inspected for sex (which one never gets to experience anyway), lips peeled back to inspect teeth, ears tested for reversibility. So until Dick and Annie turned up I wore my most pathetic hang-dog look. That's when you hunch up, snuffle to sound sickly, avoid eye contact and flatten your ears out so that your head looks like a triangle.

But Dick and Annie weren't interested in The Inspection and it didn't take me long to twig that these were the humans for me. Here was a pair of suckers I could run rings around. Although I was only five weeks old I out-charmed and out-cheesecaked all my siblings in five seconds flat. They couldn't resist me.

"Ooooooohhh, isn't he cute!" gushed Annie.
Right-on, Missus! I agreed.
"Yeah, like a hair-shirt," said Dick, but I purred so loudly in his ear and gave him such a dinky little head-butt that he went all to pieces.
"But what's wrong with his tail?" he asked the 'breeder'.

"Born broken," she said. "You won't be able to show 'im." Thinking this could count against me, she offered me for sale at a discount. People are disgusting, trafficking in cats.
"I think it's cute," coo-ed Annie, and added the clincher: "I have no intention of showing our cat, I think it's humiliating."
That sealed it for me, I decided to take them.
"We'll take him," said Dick.
"Okay," said the breeder. "What are you going to call him?"
"Frank?" they said in unison, turning to me for approval.
Frank? I repeated thoughtfully. *Frank, huh? Yeah, Frank sounds kinda good . . . it's okay with me. Righty-oh, Frank it is*!
And so that's me: Frank Something-or-Other Forsythe on the official 'papers'.

I was ready to go home with them right then and there but that wasn't allowed. I had to wait till I was eleven weeks old, at which point the 'breeder' had had enough of my pestering so she rang Dick and Annie to say I was 'very lively and independent' and did they want to come and take me home?
Did they? They couldn't get there fast enough.
C'mon guys, let's go! I shouted, trying to ignore the undignified exchange of money and 'papers'.
"Okay, Frank, keep your shirt on," said Dick. "Just let me get the cage."
Cage? Did you say ***CAGE****?*
Now there is only one foul, four-letter word in my vocabulary and that is C-A-G-E. It was time for Lesson Number One. The instant Dick made the mistake of trying to stick me in a C-A-G-E, I went berserk: howling, scratching, threatening, swearing, begging, sticking my arms and legs through the rotten thing and generally creating a MAJOR fuss.
"Now, now Frank," admonished Dick sternly. "Settle down."
Well, my motto is 'start as you mean to continue' and if these

two were ever to be trained properly, I must start immediately.
LET ME OUTTA HERE OR I'LL KILL YOU!
"Don't be silly, Frank, you're too small."
I'LL KILL YOU WHEN I GROW UP THEN!
He laughed, the stupid lout laughed. I stuck my front paws out between the bars, grabbed his finger, pulled it into my mouth and sunk my teeth in. I was very small and it didn't hurt much but he got the message.
"Hey, Frank! What's with you?"
LET ME OUTTA THIS STINKING, ROTTEN CAGE!
"Dick, that's a terrible racket he's making, try taking him out and see what happens," said Annie.
"Cats don't like cars," said Dick.
I do.
"Try 'im."
Dick took me out and sat me on his knee. As soon as he did I reverted to my normal angelic self.
"He seems to like it," said Dick, surprised.
"Oh, well, leave him out then."

I have to say they were fast learners. I was pleased with them so I gave them each a little pat on the hand with my paw which sent them into paroxysms of delight. Easily pleased, humans, easily pleased.

'Brisbane Drama' 2

My first Drama took place about ten days after I took over the household. Actually the Drama was not really mine at all, but Annie and Dick's ....

I'd had no trouble adapting to my new home and was raring to go everywhere. I was still very small, too small to go up stairs or outside or to cause much damage. But not too small to get lost. One day we drove to Brisbane, a trip I enjoyed, and stayed at our little city flat near the railway line. But I was a bit tired by the time we arrived so I immediately looked for somewhere nice to sleep. Dick and Annie were scuttling in and out with bags and stuff so I climbed onto a dining chair that was wedged tightly under the table and went sound asleep. Suddenly a voice penetrated my slumber.
"Where's Frank?"
Dead silence.
"Where's *Frank?*"
I could almost hear Dick rolling his eyes.
"I dunno."

Then there were a lot of scuffling, shuffling noises and grunts that gradually escalated to whimpers of panic.
" 'E's not here. 'E's *gone*!!"
"He just have got out the door!"
"Oh, my God, ***no***!!!"
I heard the door bang as they shot outside. I sighed and went back to sleep.

It must have been about an hour later when I heard them come in. I could hear Annie crying and blathering away.
"My poor little baby, he's all alone in the world. Someone'll steal him. He's lost, he'll starve to death. He's too young to fend for himself. He'll get run over by a car. By a ***bus***. By a ***TRAIN***! He'll be frightened and lost and crying. Oooohh, my poor little baby, he's going to be killed. God I feel awful, he's so tiny, he's so vulnerable, it's so terrible. I'll never be able to sleep at night, I'll never forgive myself, I'll be haunted by his dear little face forever."
Obviously with this racket going on I wasn't going to be able to get any more sleep so I stood up, stretched and stuck my head up over the table.
Gidday. What's going on?
Her eyes bulged and her mouth fell open.
"What are you doing ***there***?"
I live here. Or at least I do when I'm in Brisbane.
"My baby, my baby, we've found you!"
She grabbed me and hugged me almost to death.
Okay, okay take it easy. I pushed her away.
"Frankie, baby, we've been looking for you everywhere!"
Why?
"We thought you were lost. We've had all the neighbours from the other units searching the streets and railway tracks and back yards and everything. We've been ***desperate***."

I've been asleep.

"He's been there asleep all the time," said Dick, shaking his head in wonder. "We'd better let everyone know. Then I'm gonna have a drink. I feel exhausted."

"God, I feel like a real goof," said Annie.

That was the first time I heard her say that, but it certainly wasn't the last.

I can understand you feeling that way. You've made quite an ass of yourself, haven't you? I feel fine. What's for dinner? Wouldn't mind a bit of a game, what about you?

"Frank, please don't ever do that again, will you?"

If you say so, but I really didn't do anything, did I?

"I mean, you could have meowed or something. You are going to be a good little boy, aren't you Frankie?"

Oh, yes, Missus. I'm going to be a good little boy, I am!

'The Accident' 3

Annie and Dick and I were just getting to be a family when they suddenly up and dumped me in a cattery and went away for Christmas. It was pathetic, here I was, not even six months old and abandoned already. Actually I wasn't there for very long because they had arranged for our friends Cally and Jim to baby-sit our house and kitten-sit me while they were gone.

Cally and Jim were groovy. Dick and Annie left a list of instructions about me and Cally and Jim ignored them. That was the beginning of my marathons. Now that I was a big kitten, I needed to check out the environs. The trouble was, I'd be so tired by the time I got somewhere I didn't have the energy to go back home. That's how the phone calls started. I'd have to go and knock on some stranger's door and get them to phone home for Cally and Jim to come and get me. At first it went something like this.
"You got a cat named Frank?"
"Yes, why, where is he?"
"North Beach."

"My God, how did he get there?"
And they'd jump in the car and rush to get me. After this happened half a dozen or so times it became more like:
"You got a cat named Frank?"
"Where the hell is he now?"
"We found him playing with the kids in the South Beach Sandpit. Why, has he done this before?"
"Huh, you could say so."
I liked the sandpit. The kids were fine but the mothers were even better. They'd get clucky and feel sorry for me and cuddle me. I l-o-o-ve being cuddled! One day one mother even carried me all the way home trailing her kids behind her up the hot hill road. I didn't have the heart to tell her I was perfectly okay to walk.

Anyway, this pattern was well established by the time Annie and Dick came back from hols. I missed Cally and Jim and cried when they left but I got over it. Especially when Dick an' Annie gave me a big chunk of fresh fish and some of my favourite, wildly expensive, little round bikkies.

But then it happened. The Accident.

I'd gone to visit a moggie mate a few doors down. We were lying in the driveway just chewing the fat as they say, when suddenly WHAMMO! Me mate's human drove straight over me in her car. I tell you it was bloody awful! Anyway she went berserk with shock at what she'd done and carried me carefully home. Annie and Dick suspected a broken leg. They gave me some shock remedy and rushed me down to Charles, my Consulting Veterinarian.

Now I'd met Charlie before when I'd had my 'flu shots so I knew he was an okay sort of bloke, totally loopy of course, but nevertheless quite enlightened. (They do say there's a fine line between insanity and genius). Anyway, the rotten car had crushed my pelvis. I was a mess and it was a long road to Welldom. First I had to spend two weeks with Charlie. Then, when I was finally allowed home, I was confined to barracks – a large run with absolutely nothing to jump on – for the next three months. I was barely six months old and it is a tribute to my excellent character that I never complained (I am – I have to say – an exceptionally sweet natured cat).

There were compensations. During this time I acquired a taste for high quality, full bodied Australian red wines (I now drink whites too but am very discriminating as to quality). I will never forget Dick's and Annie's faces the night of my first drink. Clever Dick dipped his finger in the luscious stuff and held it under my nose as a bit of a dare. *Smart-arse*, I thought and licked it. And, by crikey, I had to admit it wasn't half bad, either.
"Did ya see that?" they ga-gaaaed to each other, and did it again. I licked it thoroughly off again. Dick kept going until all ten fingers had been licked almost skinless.
"Takes after us," he said with a note of wonder in his voice. It was an almost spiritual moment; we three were truly bonded, a family at last, joined by a deep respect for good plonk.

Even when I was allowed out I limped for a long time. It was about this time that Dick and Annie got the ridiculous idea of trying to train me to walk on a leash. HA! I put a halt to that rubbish quick smart with Lesson Number Two: Passive Resistance. As soon as they put the leash on, I flopped over on my side and lay doggo like one of those great big boneless jellyfish. They stood me up again on all-fours and gave the leash a little tug, at which I fell over and lay doggo again. So then they stood me up again, gave the leash a tug and over I fell again, lying doggo. Stand me up, tug the leash, fall over, lie doggo; all I had to do was fall down every time they put it on. They took quite a bit of de-programming but I am a most patient cat. The process went something like this:

Cajoling:
"C'mon Frankie boy, let's go walkies!" (Stand me up, tug.)
Don't make me puke. (Fall over, lie doggo.)

Begging:
"C'mon Fraaaaank . . . pulleezze . . . just try, you never know, you might like it." (Stand me up, tug.)
No way, Jose! (Fall over, lie doggo.)

Assertive:
"C'mon Frank, you're doing it on purpose. Be a good boy, walk!" (Stand me up, tug.)
Get a life! (Fall over, lie doggo.)

Impatient:
"C'mon Frank, give it a go!" (Stand me up, tug.)
I've got all day and tomorrow and the next and the one after that, how long've you got? (Fall over, lie doggo).

Exasperated:
"C'mon Frank, we haven't got all day!" (Stand me up, tug.)
Bingo! (Fall over, lie doggo.)

Angry:
"C'mon Frank, are you stupid or what?" (Stand me up, tug.)
Don't descend to their level, I told myself, just answer the question. *What.* (Fall over, lie doggo.)

Totally fraught and overwrought:
"C'mon Frank, just bloody do it! (Stand me up, tug).
Nope. (Fall over, lie doggo.)

Eventually, as I predicted, the silly pair got tired of standing me up long before I got tired of falling over.

Terminally frustrated:
"You're not bloody gonna do it, are you Frank?"
How'd you guess?
"He's not gonna do it."
"I know."
"May as well forget it."

Triumphant:
YESSS!

They took off the lead. I stood up and stretched out my front legs which is my signal to be picked up.
"You bloody stubborn cat."
Awww, don't feel too bad, you two, you gave it your best shot!
"Maybe we can try again sometime . . . ."
Oh YEAH? Just you try! Two chances you've got – Buckley's and none!
They laughed.
"Only joking Frank, only joking."

'Ernestine' 4

Things were going great. The training of my humans was well under way, my pelvis was healing and even though my rear end looked a bit mashed (and still does) most of the pain was gone. I was back to doing the rounds and marathons, making heaps of friends and generally sorting out the pecking order on the hill. Mike was still King Cat of the hill at that time even though he was pretty old and I was his Second-In-Charge. He was training me to take over for when he went to Catheaven. Everything was hunky-dory . . . that is . . . until . . . . you won't BELIEVE what they did next.

My harebrained humans somehow got the idea that if one cat was a good thing, two must be twice as good.

I was ten months old when they brought Ernestine home. Ernie was my half sister – same Dad, different Mum. We looked alike except for the fact that I grinned and she pouted and was ultra-ultra-pretty. People reckoned they couldn't tell us apart but for pete's sake by this time my trademark broken tail and sandwich-style pelvis should have made it obvious who was who.

Ernestine was a real *girl*. She was always wanting to do girl things like have deep and meaningful conversations, wash me and snuggle up. She was shy with everyone but me. You'd think she owned me the way she carried on. *You're a mess Frank,* she'd say in that tut-tut way of hers and she'd start grooming me like mad. (Actually I really enjoyed it but it doesn't do to let on about things like that or you might get the reputation of being a bit of a poofy cat.) She followed me everywhere and could sometimes be such a little madam that I'd have to smack her. She'd stir me up by running behind me and nipping at my ankles and wouldn't let up until I hit her. Then of course she'd pretend to be all wide-eyed Miss Innocence with a "What Did I Do?" type look.

Ernie irritated me but we had some terrific times together. One of our favourite things was to drive Annie and Dick to despair by proving false the crazy idea that cats are careful with fragile objects. We developed our own special game of chase. The idea was to tear at top speed across as many surfaces with the greatest number of breakable objects on them as possible. It was terrific! Middle of the night was the best time to play and breaking glassware produced the most satisfying reaction, especially if the sideboard had just been waxed. We'd go like the clappers, skidding on the slippery surfaces and whoosh! whoosh! whoosh! send all these precious little objects d'art sailing through the air before crashing to the floor in a thousand pieces! Ernie was very fast. I was a bit slower on account of my pelvis but we could still cover all the surfaces in the lounge, entry, dining room and kitchen in less than twenty seconds before flying up the stairs to the bedrooms. Dick had a huge long row of CDs sitting on a bookshelf and if we got it just right we could send the whole lot clattering to the floor in a huge jumbled heap with just one paw swipe.

Another thing we liked to do was bring presents home for our humans. They always got a good reaction, especially snakes. Dick and Annie were real funny when it came to snakes. Ernie was efficient with snakes but I was pretty sloppy which used to drive her nuts. *Frank!* she'd declare, exasperated. *How many times must I tell you, grab them just behind the head at the back of the neck!* But I just used to grab whatever bit was going past at the time. Mostly it was the middle and then I'd have trouble squeezing me and a snake bent double through the cat door. But oh, God, humans are funny! One time I brought in a long thin one. Dick had bare feet and he shot up the air and leapt all over the furniture shouting and carrying on. I kept following him around with this ruddy snake in my mouth and he's bellowing, "OH GOD, FRANK! GET THAT BLOODY THING OUTTA HERE!!" and he's leaping and hopping and running from room to room – almost as fast as Ernie and me having a good chase! Laugh! I was laughing so hard I dropped the thing out of my mouth. Annie heard the fracas and came to see what was going on and stood there gawping not knowing whether to laugh too. Anyway the snake went away out the door on its own. Not much of a sense of humour, snakes.

One day when Ernie and I were playing, we got a bit rough. She swiped me across the eye. It *rooly* hurt. It wouldn't stop running and I had to keep it closed. We had to go and see Charlie again. He squeezed my eye open. I damn near hit him. He's always giggling nervously and saying, "Sorry ol' fella." But to tell you the truth, I don't think it's us animules that put him off, I think he's more nervous of our human minders. I tell you, there's a lot of tragedy and drama gets played out in a vet clinic. Charlie looked crestfallen. "His cornea's been pierced. We can save the eye but he will only have a bit of peripheral vision left. Leave 'im here, we'll sedate 'im and stitch up his eye so that it can have a chance to heal. Come and get 'im tomorrow." So I had three weeks of one eye all stitched shut. It healed okay, but to this day I have to be terribly careful about jumping up on things in case I miss. Like the time I miscalculated and fell in the spa-pool. Oh well, it's all water under the bridge now.

Although she often drove me nuts, Ernie and I shared the same sense of humour and nearly always the same bed. I loved sleeping with her, she smelled so good. Dick said she smelled like caramel. Annie said I smelled like a horse.

Ernestine was killed on the main road on 8th November 1996. Nothing prepared me for the pain of her loss. Annie and Dick told me she'd gone to Catheaven but I didn't believe them at first. I couldn't eat or sleep and I kept looking for her everywhere for ages and ages. I was so sad and lost. We'd had a real love-hate relationship but she was still my girl and we always slept and laughed together. I went into deep depression. I didn't know how much I loved her until she wasn't there. As a mark of respect, after she died I took Ernie's name; that's how come I'm Frank *E.* Forsythe.

Ernestine

'Disappearing Acts' 5

ACT I

I was inconsolable for about six weeks, yet as time went on Ernie's death actually brought Annie and Dick and me closer. For a time Annie became overprotective. Although she tried not to worry about me too much, she sure would get twitchy if I wasn't home on time. She was such a goof that for a while whenever I was late home she'd get in the car and drive around to see if I was lying squasho on the road somewhere. So the first time I really ***didn't*** come home you can imagine how her imagination worked overtime.

What happened was I got locked in the garage of a holiday unit next door when the people who were renting it went away. I was in a bit of a pickle that's for sure. The only light came from this weenie little window way up high. I eventually managed to get up there and sit on the ledge but the window itself was closed tight and very dirty.

I had been there for over twenty-four hours when I saw Annie ploughing through the undergrowth in our back yard. I yelled

at her and banged on the window but she didn't hear me. I could see her mouthing, "Frank-Frank, Frankeeeeeeeee!" and I yelled back but she still didn't hear. I could tell she was desperate. Suddenly she burst into tears and went all disconsolate and weepy and ineffectual and ***wet***. *Bloody hell, woman*! I thought. *Just look up*. And I ***willed*** her to look up. And blow me if she didn't! I wish I'd had a camera. Her mouth fell open and her eyes just about popped their sockets. She started jumping up and down and waving her arms around and she rushed over and put her face up against the window.
Just get me out of here! I yelled. I was ***dying*** to go to the loo.

ACT II

Then there was this other time. There's a little brick house on the other side of us which the owners, who lived elsewhere, were trying to sell. One day the real estate agent came to show some people inside. As it was a while since I'd been able to make Daily Inspection in there, naturally I went to check it out too. I was out the back examining the plumbing when I heard the door slam. The lame-brains had gone and shut me in. I banged on the door and shouted but no-one heard. Night came and I could hear Annie snuffling and calling and whimpering outside and flashing a torch uselessly into the night sky. She means well but she can be a real goof at times. The next afternoon the owners turned up – a great relief for me I can tell you. Annie saw them and came over to say hello and tell them the sad news of my disappearance. There I was standing in the window not five metres away shouting and tapping like mad. Suddenly Gerry caught sight of me in the window.
"What's that, then?" I saw him mouth, pointing a startled finger at me. Everyone swung around.
"Oh, Frankie, my darling Frankeeeeeeeee!" squealed Annie.

ACT III

Now I must tell you about the best disappearing act of all. In fact, you'll be quite surprised to learn it doesn't involve me, but my predecessor. Quite a long time before I was born, Annie lived with a moggie named Jessie. One day, Annie told me this long tall tale about Jessie and she swears it is true.

They once lived in a town house in Brisbane and next door to them a new town-house was being built. It was a cavity brick building and not long before it was completed Jessie went in to investigate things and check on progress. There were a few bricks missing from the outside wall because one of the tradesmen had something or other to finish before putting the final bricks in. Anyway, as Annie tells it, that night Jessie didn't turn up for dinner, nor did she appear for breakfast the next day. The tradesmen came and went and the bricks were inserted and cemented in. By the evening of the second day, Annie and Dick were getting pretty worried so they went out with a torch calling lunatically as only humans can. They reckoned they could here a faint meowing from the house next door. So they forced the lock and went in to look. But it was dark and they weren't sure. Eventually they went home to a restless night's sleep. The next morning they got up at dawn and went back to search. Sure enough, faint, meowing sounds of life. Would you believe it? Poor old Jess had got into the brick cavity and been cemented in.

The workmen arrived. The brickie was a total creep. "I'm not gunna jack-hammer me brickwork out just for a bloody cat!" Annie said even at that hour of the morning he had bad B.O. and it seemed like an ill-wind, as they say. But then the foreman arrived. "Well, if we leave the bloody thing in there it'll die and stink and no-one'll buy the place." And so, with such humanitarian, pragmatic motivation the bricks were laboriously removed and Jessie was home in time for breakfast. I understand her only other claim to fame except for longevity was an engaging ability to sit in the laundry tub and blow gently into the water spout at just the right angle to make it whistle!

Once I went away for two whole nights and two whole days but I can't tell you where I was 'cause it's a secret. You don't need me to tell you what Annie was like when I got home, do you?

'How I Keep Charlie Solvent' 6

SCENE I

One day when I was a bit bored I thought it might be interesting to go down and count the cars on the highway outside the hardware store. I got up to 467 and somehow lost concentration. The next thing I knew I was being skittled, flung in the air by a speed-freak and sent skidding across the bitumen. I made the mistake of trying to slow the skid by digging in my claws but all that happened was a very short claw-cut. The hardware store man raced out and picked me up. We went and phoned Annie. I had tyre marks on my sides and head and Annie said I smelled like burnt rubber. Yuk, makes me feel dizzy just talking about it. Annie rushed me at a thousand miles an hour down the highway to see my mate, Charlie, the mad, clever vet.

"Jeez, ol' fella," exclaimed Charlie. "Whatcher been doing now?" He poked and prodded and then he laughed and produced the only major damage which was the bill. Nothing broken except the tip of a tooth. Oh well, nothing dentured, nothing deigned!

SCENE II

By now I had outgrown my little kitten-sized scratch pole so Dick and I decided to build a new one. It turned out fantastic. It's about four feet high and sits up against the stairs overlooking the kitchen where I can see everything. We put a great little seat on the top and all. Ernie and I would wedge there together when she was little but as she grew older she would push me off. Anyway, one day as I was industriously stripping the loose carpet off the side, Dick tickled me under the armpits. He found a lump.

"Come-an'-have-a-look-at-this," he said to Annie. They put on their glasses and turned me upside down and checked out my armpit.

"Do you think it's a tick?"

"I dunno, do *you* think it's a tick?"

"I dunno."

"Me neither."

"What'll we do?"

"Pull it off?"

"S'pose we could give it a try."

"Righty-oh. I'll hold him, you pull it off."

"No, I'll hold him, *you* pull it off."

"I don't know what I'm doing."

"Well, neither do I."

"Well, for God's sake, give 'im here to me."

Someone pulled it.

Ouch! I'm outa here.

I jumped down and moved quickly out of reach. They stood like stuffed dummies peering at me thoughtfully through their glasses.

The next morning I felt crook. Annie took me to see Charlie, the loony, laughing vet. Charlie gets bad hay fever. He sneezes like mad and it's a wonder he can see anything what with his nose pouring and his eyes streaming. Anyway, he said, "Bloody hell, you've left the head in!" Now any idiot knows ***you never leave the head in***. Annie reckoned she felt like a real idiot and said so. "God, I feel like a real idiot."

"You'll have to leave him here," said Charlie. "I'm going to have to anti-thingumy him. We've ***probably*** caught it in time. But I'll have to watch him for the next twenty-four hours."

Probably?

I survived. You know what they say: 'A tick in time saves nine'!

SCENE III

The day I stuck my head out the front door and didn't feel like going out, I knew I was sick, sick, sick. Getting outside is my favourite thing to do, ***second*** thing in the morning. First favourite thing is to get a cuddle in bed with Annie and Dick. I bang on the bedroom door about six-thirty and they hafta get up and let me in, otherwise I rattle it so hard they can't sleep anyway. Dick gets up and opens the door and I find a patch of sunshine on the rug and let him give me a good rub. Then he yawns and says, "Well Frank, it's time I got us a cuppa tea, go and visit Annie." Annie's always still dozing but I fix that quick. I walk right up her legs and stand on her stomach and knead her 'chest' and rattle-purr wetly into her ear. I whistle a bit in the process and she always starts to laugh. Then we have this thing where I try to get between the sheets and she tries to stop me. "Get outa here, Flea-bag," she always says. I don't take it too hard on account of I've got no fleas and she knows it 'cause they're always de-flea-ing me.

Anyway, this day I felt pretty wobbly. I went upstairs and slept all morning on the verandah. By the afternoon Dick and Annie were starting to get worried. "He's never this well behaved,"

they whispered furtively to each other. "There must be something wrong with him." In the evening, Dick offered me some wine but I couldn't raise the slightest interest. Next day I hadn't moved, so they took me down to see Charlie.
"Frank," he said, "You sick AGAIN?"
Uh huh.
"Speak to me, Frank!"
But I was that crook, all I could do was croak. Charlie was shocked. "Frank, my buddy, you are shockingly sick. We're gonna have to get serious." Charlie uses any excuse to stick a thermometer up my bum and this occasion was no exception. But this time I was too sick even to smack him. Another fact which didn't escape his notice.
"He didn't even pat me like he usually does. And he has one hell of a temperature. He sure is one sick puppy."
Pussy, *if you don't mind,* I objected as vehemently as I could but it sounded pathetic.
"Yeah, mate, figure of speech. Sorry. ***Pussy***." Charlie then announced that I had 'a massive infection from an unknown cause'. You know, vets must get fantastic training to be able to come up with such an astute diagnosis, don't you reckon? He gave me a big needle but I didn't even care.
"You must nurse him carefully," he told Dick and Annie. "And give him all these pills."

I nearly carked it, you know. But Annie and Dick clucked and fussed and cried and told me what wonderful a cat I was (which was hardly news to me, of course) and how much they needed me and how lost they'd be without me.
Will you always be nice to me and give me anything I ask for?
"Frank, don't we always give you the best of everything?"
No.
"Don't we always buy you the best food and drink, supply

you with the most up-market accommodation and ensure you have the best life-style possible?"
No, not as I see it.
"What can we do to make you better?"
Gimme some of those wildly expensive little round bikkies.
"I know," said Dick. "Let's give him those wildly expensive little round bikkies."
Good boy, Dick.

And so, eventually, with pills, tiny tit-bits, TLC and those wildly expensive little round bikkies, I rallied. Of course I had to be hand-fed for a while, taking a little wine for my stomach's sake and sleeping between the sheets. But I lived to tell the tail ... TAIL – get it? Ha ha. And in the end I got bored and announced to the world I was ready to take it on:

Gidday world, it's me – Frank E!
Here I come, come, come,
Once more into the fray
On this gorgeous Sunshine Coasty Day!

And off I sped across the road, down the hill and ran smack-bang straight into .... ***Trouble***. What else?

SCENE IV

Hot on the heels of this nearly-being-dead business, just a few blissful, glowing mornings later I set forth full of *joie de vivre* to see what the day had in store. But danger lurked abroad. Unknown to me, skulking amongst the bushes in the embankment on the other side of the road was a wild cat looking for trouble. Suddenly, before you could even say Frank-the-Fearless, this ill-mannered, maverick lout spotted me and sprang. The ratbag went straight for my jugular which he

fortunately missed but nevertheless got me under the chin, piercing right through into my mouth!
AAAAGGGGH! I yelled in shock and horror. *BUGGEW-OFF-OO-PWICK*! But it was me who got outta there in a hurry. I was pretty angry. There I was minding my own business and this interloping creep attacked me. ON MY TERRITORY! Normally I'm not one to make a fuss, but this time I went straight home and told Annie.
Wook, Annie, a wotten wile-cat dit ne in ny nouth!
"Oh no, Frank E! Have you been fighting ***again***?!"
Dann it Annie! How can you ewen tink dat? Where'd your heart? I'n your innotent wittle doy!
"How can you stand there looking so innocent, Frank?"
I ***an*** *innotent! I wad jut ninding ny own duidnett an' dit dahtahd dit ne. Don't jut 'tand dere, Annie, do tunting!*
"Charlie . . . AGAIN."

So, off we went to Charlie of course.
"Gidday, Frank."
Gidday, Tarlie.
"What's wrong, Frank?"
Dere'd a nean, watdag wile-cat down de endanknent an' I wad jut goin' tor a wittle 'troll an it attacked ne. I didn't do nutting.
"Oh, yeah?"
What'd wong wit all o' you? I'n telling you de trut'. I' you don't deliede ne, tee what I care. Jut tut-ut an' doh to duggery! An' you earn your ruddy tee, Tarlie, and tix ne ut good!

"Okay ol' fella, come here and let's have a look." He prised open my jaw and peered in. His great fist was like a gob-stopper in my mouth. "Yup, he really gotcha, didn't he mate?" He was behaving just like those idiot dentists who ask you questions when your mouth is wide open. Naturally I couldn't answer him so I squeezed his hand by way of reply. With my claws. And my jaws.

AAAARGGGH!! shouted Charlie.

Dat'll teat you to doubt ny word, Tarlie ol' nan. What a performance he put on.

'Top tnivelling, I admonished him but then when he kept blathering I added soothingly, *Jut tink od de nonney, ol' tun, jut tink od de nonney.*

'Bad Day in Paradise' 7

All week it had been raining, raining, raining. Then Friday dawned and promised to be a glorious day. A Sunshine Coast winter morning is about the most beautiful thing in the world. Warm golden sun, blue roaring ocean, white clean sand, cool breeze, flowers smelling fresh and looking pretty, birds making a racket in the trees. Nice.

Annie says I have to tell you this story because it'll help you understand why sometimes she gets exasperated with me. It's not really my fault. Anyway, this day, Annie had to go to town to get a new ink cartridge for my computer (my memoirs, you understand) and to pick up some skirt or other she was having made. She'd rung the suppliers to make sure they had the right cartridge and the dressmaker to ensure the dress was ready. So off she went on the sixty km round trip. First thing that happened was that despite their assurances, the suppliers didn't have the right cartridge. Annie dug in her handbag for her wanker-phone to ring around and find someone who did. But the phone wasn't there. So then she spent the next half hour standing in a 'charmingly' scented, hot phone box rooting around for change and ringing all these shops. Finally this big office joint said they had one so off she went again, another seven kilometres down the road. Annie definitely wasn't very bright that day 'cause it wasn't until she was half way to the shop that she remembered that her wanker-phone had been in the glovebox the whole time. Anyway, it gets worse, 'cause when she ***finally*** got served after waiting ***twenty*** minutes, it turned out they didn't have the right one either! Oooh boy. Annie was getting shirty and that's something you don't really want to hang around for. She's got a long fuse but boy, when it goes, it goes! Anyhow, this big, burly, tattooed, crew-cut, body-pierced male shop assistant must've seen the steam coming outta her ears 'cause he came over to investigate the fracas. Patiently he listened to the saga. "You must be real pissed-off, eh love?" he observed sympathetically. Annie was mollified by his sensitivity and even more so when he got on the phone and rang around all these places and finally found her a cartridge. The only hitch was it was ***another*** ten kilometres down the road. Nevertheless, off she went.

This time she got the cartridge alright, but by now it was getting late and she still had to drive back to the dressmaker's shop. She managed to get there just before it shut. But, just as she was about to take the skirt and hand over the money, something made her try the darn thing on first for size. Apparently she looked like high tide at Alexandra Headland. Billows and ripples everywhere.
"Look at it!" she wailed. The shop lady stuck her head on the side and yanked the skirt this way and that.
"It's the material," she said.

"I don't give a damn what it is," said Annie. "If it's not fixed I'm not paying!"
"I'll fix it," said the shop lady. "Go and do something for half an hour."

Annie walked outside. It was after five, the shops were shut except for the florist who was doing a roaring pre-Mother's Day sale. She was loitering vacantly on the footpath when her (rediscovered) wanker-phone burped. It was a friend of hers in tears. Some old boyfriend trouble or other. Annie was sympathetic. "I'll come around and commiserate over a drink with you when I get home," she promised. Then, while she was still waiting for the skirt, she thought it might be nice to buy her friend some flowers. So off she went into the florist's. Because it was so busy she had to wait about ten minutes but finally she got served.
"I want three red roses and three white ones nicely tarted up," she told the pregnant shop assistant. Fifteen minutes later the girl came back with six red roses nicely tarted up. "I asked for three red and three white," said Annie.
"I couldn't reach the white ones," replied the assistant airily.
"But they are right over there at eye level," protested Annie.
"Yeah, but me stomach got in the way," said the assistant, smiling apologetically and patting the complacent brat inside.
"How much is that?" Annie asked, resigned to red roses.
"Fifteen dollars," said the assistant, smiling sweetly.
"How come?" objected Annie. "The roses are only $1-50 each and this bit of green stuff can't have cost all that much!"
"Ah no, the white ones are $1-50, the red ones are $2-00 each."

She went back to the shop and tried on the skirt again. Medium tide at Alex. She couldn't be bothered arguing although she knew she'd probably never wear it. Just get home, she thought, feed Frank (me), take the roses to the friend and have a glass of plonk to commiserate.

Well, I had intended a bit of a surprise. This first sunny day out in ages and what should happen but I came across a ruddy great rat. Now, since I'd been lying around for two or three weeks and felt pretty buoyed up by the lovely weather, I decided to take him on. He was *big*. Nevertheless, I managed to get him around the neck, drag him in through the cat door and all the way upstairs, and chuck him on the Turkish rug. There I dealt with him properly: wrestling, biting, clawing and shaking him to smithereens, yet he still managed to sink his enormous great fangs into my foot. Hell, it hurt! I was so mad I bit his head off. Then for good measure I disembowelled him.

After that marathon battle I went outside for some fresh air. I walked over the road to see Em. My foot was throbbing from the bite and I couldn't put any weight on it. Em picked me up. It was dusk when we saw Annie drive in. We waited until she opened the front door and put all her bits and pieces inside and then we went over. Even in the dusk I could see the look on her face. She went pale.

"Oh, God. What now? What's happened to 'im?" she screeched on a rising note of hysteria.

I've hurt my foot, I said.

"He's hurt his foot," said Em.

"Oh, for heaven's sake, gimme a look," said Annie and they tipped me upside down and peered at my pad.

"Shit," said Annie. "This is all I need, what's happened ***this*** time?"

"I dunno," said Em.

That bloody rat did it, I told them.

"What rat?" said Annie.

"What rat?" said Em.

That bugger over there, I said, pointing.
Annie spun around, peering into the gloom.
"Oh, NO, Frank! Yuk! Gross!"
What's wrong? I said, quite taken aback.
"What's WRONG?"
Well I'm blowed if I could work out what was wrong with her. It was a brilliant coup, a fantastic battle scene with blood and guts everywhere. I even got wounded in the process. Wearily she put me down and went for some paper to clean up the rat.
"Don't forget the head," said Em, supervising from a safe distance. "It's over there."
I shook my head in bewildered disappointment.
I'm outta here, I said forlornly and limped into the hot water cupboard.
Annie disposed of my trophy and went out.

By the time she came home an hour later, I was feeling *rooly* crook. Couldn't stop shaking. Then she felt guilty for going out. She tried to phone Charlie-the-Vet on his after hours number but it wasn't answering. So then she rang another vet. He was drunk. So she rang another one. He shouted over the phone, "I've just been bitten by a bloody cat, me hand's all swelled up and right now the last thing I want to see is another damn cat!" Then she rang a woman vet who must've been in bed with some bloke 'cause there was a man saying sexy things in the background and she didn't want to see me. At nine o'clock Annie gave up. She got a sheepskin rug and a lovely soft old flannelette sheet, some disinfectant and some strange homoeopathic stuff. First she disinfected my foot. Then she put the sheepskin on the big lounge chair and stuck me and my throbbing foot on it. Then she snuggled the sheet around me and stuck this stuff in my mouth. The throbbing stopped, I felt warm, protected, loved. I went to sleep. The last thing I heard

was the popping of a wine cork and Annie muttering:
"What a shit of a day."

I felt much better the next morning, but my paw still hurt so off we went to see Charlie. "His leg's all swelled up," said Charlie observantly, with a big grin. A thermo up the bum, a needle, a tablet, some special biscuits to cheer me up, some ripper-dooley flea stuff and off we went home. All's swell that ends swell! Eighty-four bucks. No wonder Charlie laughs a lot.

'Poverty of Spirit' 8

Life's a bugger. All I was doing was cat-things. Perfectly natural, perfectly normal cat things, yet those silly dumb humans have gone and made me feel like a criminal. All I did was go and say hi to the new neighbours. There was this big bloke with pecs like Mohammed Ali, a lady and a baby. Just hello, that's all. And since they didn't answer when I knocked at the front door, naturally I went around the back. And since there was a window open at the back, naturally I hopped in.

Well, you should have seen the sight that met my eyes. Two poor little budgies locked up in a cage on the top of a wardrobe. It was a pathetic sight, my heart bled for them cooped up like that. I had to do something.

Don't worry little birds, I'm Frank the Fearless, I'll rescue you! I cried. With a heroic leap I sprang to the top of the wardrobe and swept the cage to the floor. The cage door burst open and out came the budgies. One fluttered down behind the wardrobe where I couldn't reach it but the other started flapping and squawking like a demented thing. Well, *naturally* I had to restrain it until it calmed down a bit, and *naturally* I didn't want to hurt it with my claws so the only other option was to put my mouth over it. But you wouldn't read about it – instead of calming down the stupid thing went crazy! So *naturally* I had to kind of hold it more firmly with my teeth. The more it squawked, of course, the firmer I held it. Finally it went quiet and I was able to let it go, but oh my, you would not believe it! The bloody thing was dead!

So *then* what was I supposed to do? I certainly couldn't risk upsetting the new neighbours by confronting them with a dead budgie when they got home, could I? I had to think creatively and in the end I decided the best thing to do was get rid of the body so I picked it up and took it outside. But then what? I couldn't bury it, could I? There really was nothing left for me to do but eat it. So *naturally* that's what I did!

It was very unfortunate that Dick caught me with some tell-tale feathers in my whiskers. He started on at me about it, but at the time he didn't realise it was next door's bird. Until that night, that is. There I was, just settling down with my cabernet-merlot when there was this *bang-bang-bang* at our door. Oh, hell no! It was the bloke with big pecs from next door. Ever so quietly I slipped into the hot water cupboard while the shit hit the fan.

Our new neighbour's name was Brian but he didn't spend much time on formalities. In fact he got right to the point pretty quick: "Your bloody cat ate our budgie and the other one's so upset he's gonna die!" I tried not to listen. It was awful. Annie was trying to apologise and calm everything down and finally she was 'invited' next door to inspect the damage and meet his wife, Judy, who was crying like anything. After twenty minutes or so I heard Annie coming back up the stairs and I squigged

down even smaller. But she was on to me, there was no escape.
"Frank!" she said, deadly serious. I could tell I was for it.
"Frank! Come out here please, *at once*!"
Sheeeit.
"Frank, are you going to come out or do I have to come and get you?"
Okay, okay, keep your shirt on.

I emerged with my head and tail high, a cat condemned without fair trial, proud and cavalier in the face of impending monstrous injustice. As I said before, she made me feel like a criminal. However, I am proud to report that although I got ***very*** seriously 'spoken to' I managed to retain my composure and dignity throughout the whole ghastly ordeal.
Do I have right of reply? I asked when she ***finally*** finished.
"No."
But I absolutely insist. That place is a cat's smorgasbord: two budgies – well, one now – three fish and a pet rat. I ask you, what kind of absurdity is it keeping a pet rat? You know what a splendid ratter I am. Your expectations of my self-restraint are unreasonable. I demand a fair trial.
"Frank, all you're gonna get is a fair warning."
The justice system in this household stinks.
"Tough."

It died the next day, the other budgie that is, and a few days after that Annie and Judy went shopping for another couple of birds. To show that there were no ill-feelings I offered to go with them to help choose. They refused. Poverty of spirit I call that, poverty of spirit.

'Bad Boy Frank' 9

Well, they went and got another birdie. One big one instead of two small ones. Brian and Judy (we were all friends by now and knew each others' names and everything) were pretty good about letting me visit still. They had forgiven me completely seeing as how I ***accidentally*** got rid of their budgies. Anyway, this day I went over for Daily Inspection and to check out the new bird. Annie had got them a proper chain to hang the cage from the ceiling where I couldn't reach it. I strolled inside, jumped up on the couch so's I could see properly and gazed up at the new bird. It sure was a pretty sight.

That's a nice looking bird you've got there, Judy, I remarked conversationally. *What is it?*
"A cockatiel, Frank."
I don't suppose . . . do you think it might like to play with me, Jude?
"No, Frank, I do not. In fact I'd like you to keep away from it."
Ah, Jude . . . . actually, I can't. I've . . . I've got this kind of addiction. You know, like smoking and gambling and drinking and so on. Only with me it's birds.

"Frank E., I like you very much but I'd like you to keep your addictions out of our house."
Well, it was hard, but I sure did like Judy a lot so I did my best to shut my eyes during Daily Inspection (which is a bit stupid when you think about it!) or whenever else I went into their house.

Then, one afternoon when I was dozing on our verandah, I saw Judy bring the birdcage outside. Well blow me if she didn't take the bird out and sit it on her shoulder while she proceeded to hose out the cage. Now anyone who's ever had an addiction knows what it's like, and just like a gambler, I couldn't resist a little flutter . . . in my case the feathered variety. I saw Judy look up and she looked me in the eye and went on hosing. How could I . . . .? Hang on! She'd said to keep my addictions out of their *house*, not out of their *yard*! Whoopeeee! I was off, down the stairs, over the garden wall and LEAP!!! Up I went, high, high in the air and bingo! I picked it right off her shoulder and took off. Back over the garden wall, up the stairs and nearly through the cat door when AAARRRGH!!! ME TAIL!!! Judy had chased me and grabbed me by the tail and there I was, stuck; half in, half out with a bird in my mouth.

It died. I didn't eat it or anything. When Judy started to cry, I felt like the rottenest heel in the world. Sometimes I hate myself. Not very often of course but that was a bad moment.

Now here is why Judy is one of the nicest people in the world: she forgave me. Again. But they gave up keeping birds after that. She still lets me do Daily Inspection and play with Tammy the cat and Buzz the toddler.

But not the goldfish. And not the pet rat named Barry. Pity.

Bad Boy Frank

'The Visit' 10

A couple of months ago, Annie and Dick were invited to brunch by my old mates, Cally and Jim, who'd recently bought a flash new barbecue and wanted to test-drive it. They had this cat, Maddie. 'Maddie' sure is the right name for her – cute as a button and mad as a cut snake, but I digress.

"Bring Frank E. to the barbie!" they urged. "And he can play with Maddie."

"Yeah, good idea!" enthused Dick and Annie.

"Frank E., you're coming with us to a barbecue with Cally and Jim."

Uh-oh.

Oh, no; thanks all the same.

"You'll enjoy it, Frank, you can meet Maddie and share in the barbecue."

But I've made other plans for today!

"Come here and let me tidy you up a bit," said Annie, ignoring my protest. I ducked as she came at me with a brush.

Hey, I'm okay as I am. And anyway, don't I get a say in this? I thought this was a democracy.

"It is a democracy, majority rules. Dick and I want you to come, it's two against one."
They ignored my protest and put me in the car and, being the exceptionally sweet-natured, agreeable, easy going cat that I am, I *graciously* went along with *them* and *their* plans.
Did I throw a tantrum? No.
Did I put on a sour face and try to spoil their day? No. That's me. Frank the Fair. Frank the Just. Frank the People's Hero.

We arrived amidst the usual shrieks of delight and I suffered the inevitable bosom-squeeze and perfume blast as Annie (carrying me) and Cally kissed the air near each others' ears. Then Cally introduced me to Maddie.
"Now, Frank E., this is Maddie. I'm sure you two'll get on just fine."
Well, she was so pretty I went straight over to her and introduced myself, completely oblivious to the menacing gleam in her lovely blue eyes.
Gidday, Gorgeous! I'm Frank. Let's play! I invited, and gave her a friendly cuff and a bit of a sniff. Maddie shrank back with a hostile hiss that exposed perfect pearly teeth and thrust out a pawful of elegantly manicured, unsheathed claws. Her beautiful eyes, fringed with thick black eyelashes gleamed threateningly.
Yeah? Well, ***Frank, I'm*** *Maddie, I'm beautiful, everyone says so and I'll have you know this is* ***my*** *house and what I say goes and don't you think you can come in here and start throwing* ***your*** *weight around. Got it,* ***Frank****?*
Yeah, I got it, you bloody bossy, beautiful, bad-tempered bitch.
Everyone was standing around saying dumb things like, "Now come on you two, be friends." They were eating fruit and getting out the stuff for the barbecue but since no-one offered me anything to eat, I mooched off to explore. Maddie pursued

me, blue eyes blazing furiously, grey-white fur sticking out wildly like a peacock with a crew-cut.
If you know what's good for you, ***Frank Forsythe****, you'll get outside and stay outside, and* ***don't*** *leave any 'messages' either, you skinny* ***Tom****!*

Well that was way over the top, just too damn much. The hospitality here was like poison. And as for being a *Tom*, not only was it anatomically incorrect but a totally unprovoked insult.

Now, everyone in the house had been warned that under no circumstances was I to be allowed out. But where there's a will, there's a way and I was not about to put up with any more rubbishing. I turned my rear end in her direction and let her think I was going to . . . . but said instead, *Okay you haughty bitch, if you think you're so smart, how the hell do I get out of here?* So she showed me, but if you think I'm going to reveal ***how***, forget it. Some strategies are protected by Cat Copyright.

I wandered down into the garden and tried to get some action out of a couple of pathetic lizards. But when no amount of prodding could induce them to play, I went to explore next door. That was a mistake, a very BIG MISTAKE, because *that's* when I met a really BIG DOG. Well, I won't tell you what the miserable sod threatened to do if he caught me but it was enough to make me high-tail it out of there mighty quick. But the sly, pig-eyed brute came after me and managed to corner me near the garage. The only way out was up. I fled: ears back, legs extended, tail flying, heart thumping, faster than the wind I fairly flew up the impossibly smooth, straight trunk of a very tall gum tree. I tell you, I was s . . . scared that somehow the bugger would come after me. He couldn't of course, and although he soon gave up barking insanely around the base of the tree I was so scared I froze, couldn't move a whisker.

I started to cry. What was I *doing* here? It was *their* fault. I could have been home minding my hillside, keeping order and enjoying life. Instead, here I was in alien territory, stuck up the tallest tree in the country, spurned, unwanted, unloved, lost and forgotten. I cried and cried until eventually a bloke came out of a house across the road, looked quizzically up at me and went back inside. Time passed. I was tired and hungry.

I was just about to give up hope when I heard a familiar screech.
"Aaaaaaaaaaah! Where's Frankeeee!?"
I'm up here! I'm up here!
Never was I so glad to hear Annie's histrionics but she was making such a racket no-one heard me.
"He's gone, he's gone!" she ranted comfortingly. "He's got out, my baby's gone, I'll never find 'im again, he's all alone in alien territory. Oh God, what'm I gonna do, we've gotta find 'im!" Then she yelled at Dick to stop standing there with his mouth open and DOOOO Something.
"What?" said Dick, practically.
Then I heard Cally start.
"Oh, my God, I feel awful. Stop the barbecue, Jim!"
"Why?" said Jim, practically.
"How can you think of food when Frank E.'s gone?"
"Easy," said Jim.
"We've gotta go look for him," screeched Annie and Cally in unison.
"Better on a full stomach," said Jim, practically.
"How can you *say* that?" declared Cally, outraged.
"He'll find his way back okay," said Dick hopefully.
"How can you *say* that?" declared Annie, tearfully.

This went on for a while and then, as I expected, emotion won out over reason and a search campaign was mounted. Well, I have to say it was the most disorganised hunting event I've ever witnessed and I certainly had an excellent vantage point. In fact it was so awful, now that I knew I was safe, I stopped crying and just watched. Annie went out in the car cruising the streets at snail's pace with the windows rolled down and yelling my name so loudly you could hear her way down the hillside. Cally beat her breast in self-recrimination and shuffled off down the street on foot peering hopefully into bushes, bins and backyards. Dick stood where he was with his hands on his hips calling, "Frank-Frank-Frank!" in short, staccato bursts, but not very loudly. You could tell he was embarrassed in case the neighbours heard and came out to see who the silly sod was calling like that. Jim stared mildly and aimlessly into the air, a stubby in his right hand travelling intermittently up to his mouth and down again. He was muttering consoling but ineffectual (and totally inaccurate) platitudes about my Likely Whereabouts and wondering vaguely what happened to the barbecue.

Eventually Annie and Cally returned. I could tell they were *rooly* upset. Satisfied now that the party was ruined and we would be able to go home, I was just about to yell out again when the bloke across the road, hearing Annie's caterwauling, came outside to investigate the fracas.
"You lost a cat?"
"YES!" they all cried in unison.
"Sounded like it, all that yelling and everything." He scratched his round belly through its blue singlet and bent down to flick a stone from his rubber thong with a couple of grubby fingers. He burped.
"It's up a tree."

"Where?!"

"Straight up."

Four pairs of eyes followed his pointing, ragged-nailed finger and came to rest on me.

"Aaaaaaaah! Frank E. darling!"

"There 'e is!"

"Bloody stupid cat, you had us all upset!"

"What the hell are you doing up there?"

A dog chased me up here and I couldn't get down.

"The dog from up the road chased 'im up there an hour or so ago," said the man.

"Come on down Frank-Frank," urged Dick.

No.

"Come on Frank, I'll catch you."

No, I'm not stupid, I don't trust you.

" 'E's not stupid," confirmed the man. "You won't get 'im to come down from there, the trunk's too smooth." And he laughed as he went inside.

I looked down at the four faces staring up at me.

Get a ladder why don't you?

"Where's your ladder, Jim? I'll have to go up and get him."

"Haven't got one," said Jim.

"Blast, we'll have to borrow one from somebody," said Dick and trailed off after the man. He came back with an extension ladder. He was nervous, not wanting to let on he was afraid of heights. He climbed half way up. "C'mon Frank," he pleaded hopefully. A substantial film of sweat broke out on his forehead. I thought it might be fun to lead him on a bit and started to retreat.

"You BUGGER, Frank!"

Don't speak to me like that.

"Don't frighten 'im," said Annie.

"Frighten *him* be damned!" shrilled Dick. He moved closer,

sweat trickling. Suddenly, faster than a pussy-paw, his fist shot out and clamped down on my neck.
"Gotcha!"
Hell, mate, don't drop me! I started to struggle.
"Sheee-it, Frank! Don't bloody struggle!"
The ladder started to wobble. Dick's eyes bulged, sweat poured off him and his heart was thumping so loudly I could hear it. Compassion. I put my arms around his neck and hung on tight, purring loudly into his ear to reassure him. But there's just no pleasing some people.
"F-f-f-frank, g-g-g-get ya bloody c-c-c-claws out o' me bleedin' neck!" he roared. I let go. Four people gasped simultaneously but Dick caught me just before I fell. Hero.
"Aahhhhhhhhh. . . . . ." said the little crowd.
We made it to the ground. Everyone looked rattled.
Can we go home now?
"I think we'd better go home now," said Annie. "If he can get out once, he can get out again." The three of us piled into the car. To this day I can see Jim standing in the driveway with his barbie tongs in one hand and his stubby in the other. You could tell he was at least half-an-hour behind everyone else. As we backed out of the driveway I heard him ask Cally:
"What happened to me barbie?"

'Sorting Bruce' 11

There had been serious goings-on. *Rooly* serious. I don't understand humans; one minute they are celebrating the way one is, the next, they're bemoaning it! You are aware, no doubt, that the 'one' whereof I speak is me. Let me tell you what happened.

A new neighbour had moved on to our hill. In fact, I told you about her in the beginning – Jill – remember? Anyway, being in Neighbourhood Watch, naturally I went over and introduced myself. And I discovered, much to my pleasure, that Jill-Down-The-Hill was a very nice lady.
Hi, I'm Frank E., King-of-The-Hill. Just popped down to check out your house and grounds and make sure everything's tickety-boo.
"Hi, Frank E., nice to meet you," said Jill.
Mind if I look around?
"Go ahead," said Jill. "But first I'd like you to meet my boys, Ben and Bruce."
Hey, Guys. Ben was a big handsome Tabby; Bruce a scruffy Ginger.
Just here to check things over, I assured them.

Righto, said Ben, *I'm off outside to explore. See ya.*
Yeah, see ya, Ben. Nice meeting you.
I set off down the hallway towards the bedroom.
Ah, excuse me, where do you think you're going? said a decidedly cool voice. I turned around. Bruce was standing there, just flicking his scrawny tail and watching me.
I told you already, mate, just checking things out.
Not in my house, you don't, said Bruce.
I ignored the silly sod and kept on going 'til I came to a pretty bedroom.
Hey, neat bed! I said, jumping up on the lovely white damask bedcover.
Get off Jill's bed! growled Bruce.
Ho hum, I thought, and sighing, turned patiently to face him.
You don't seem to understand, Bruce-ole-boy, I explained slowly and carefully. *This is my territory,* ***I*** *run things around here. Besides, Jill said it was okay with her.*
I made a nice little nest on the bed, lay down and stretched out.
Not in my house you don't.
I could hardly believe my ears. Who the hell did this joker think he was? He was being so absurd I decided to ignore him. Unfortunately, it was the wrong decision, for the next thing I knew he'd jumped up on the bed, seized my leg between his teeth and . . . CHOMP!! EEEYIKES! The bastard bit me! And boy, did it hurt!
Now get out, said Bruce and, since it was obvious that at that precise moment he had the upper paw, I complied.
I'm going, buster, I told him as I limped out, *but this ain't over yet, I'll deal with you later!*

I was hoping the pain would've gone by the next day but nope, I was still limping.
"What's wrong with Frank E.'s foot?" Dick asked Annie.

"Dunno, why?"
"He's limping."
And they stuck me upside down and examined each paw and all over my body for ticks.
It's not my paws, it's my leg. Look! I said, sticking out my leg.
"I can't see anything," said Annie.
It's me leg! I yelled at them as I tried to walk.
"Well, something's wrong with him, I reckon we better take him to see Charlie."
"Charlie must just ***love*** us," Annie sighed. "But I guess you're right."
So they put me in the car and off we went.
"There's something wrong with him, Charlie, he's limping, dunno why."
"Gidday, Frank E.!" said Charlie, straight up. "Whaddya done to yer leg, mate?"
Thank God ***someone's*** *got some sense,* I declared; *Bruce bit me.*
"Whew, that's quite a bite, Frank, right through from one side to the other. Who'd you stir up this time?"
Who me? I didn't do anything.
"I can't believe I didn't see that before," said Annie. "I feel like a real goof."
You are, I confirmed.
"Yeah, well," said Charlie. "His leg's swelled to about three times its normal size . . . sometimes I wonder about you two . . ."
The usual story. Hit it with mega pills to avoid an abscess and by about five days later I was right as rain. But something still had to be done to sort out that stroppy cat.

This was ***my*** hill, it was up to me to keep it that way. I couldn't let Bruce think he'd got the better of me, so I went down and engaged in a few skirmishes with the idea of teaching him a lesson.

"I can't understand it," Henry tattle-tailed to Annie. "Frank is being uncharacteristically aggressive. Something's got his dander up. He's deliberately picking fights with Bruce."
I tried to sort Henry out; really I'm amazingly patient.
Listen, Henry, I explained, *this is* ***my*** *hill. I* ***have*** *to defend my territory.* But he wouldn't listen and kept snitching on me. All this was pretty upsetting, no-one understood how important this was to me, not even my friends which rooly hurt.

Then came the cruncher. Dick and Annie went away for a couple of weeks and packed me off to Myrtle's Home for The Bewildered. (Actually I like Myrtle's cattery, but don't let on.) When I came home I discovered that during my absence that miserable brute Bruce had been marking out my territory, and not *only* my territory but *my* yard and *my* house! Wretched animal! Something had to be done. I went down to confront him.
You bloody barbarian, Bruce, you've been stealing my territory and marking ***my*** *house and* ***my*** *yard. You asked for it, I'm gonna fix you once and for all! Take that!* I took an almighty swipe at him. But I missed.
Get lost, Frank, he said.
That was it. That was damn-well IT! No-one speaks to me like that. I lunged at him with my mouth open, ready to bite. But again he was too fast. He got me first. On the face. Right through from the bottom of my cheek up to the eye. I staggered back in a haze of pain.
I'm not through with you yet, you feline menace. You'll live to regret that! I promised, though now more in hope than expectation. I staggered home.
"Hi, Frank E., whatcherdoin'?" greeted Annie. She picked me up and gave me a cuddle. "Gee Frank, you've been such a good little lad lately, no more fighting, thank heaven. Dick will be pleased to hear it when he gets home."

Oh, well, I thought, *better not say anything; it'll only get me into trouble and maybe it'll heal up on its own.*
The following evening Dick came home. "Gidday Frank E. lad," he said. "How you doin'?"
"He's been very good," said Annie. Dick picked me up for a cuddle. Suddenly he saw my face.
"My God! What's wrong with his face, it's all swelled up!"
I sighed, resigned to the fact that I wasn't going to get away with it. Besides, it hurt.
Bruce bit me.
"Did you go down there and fight with Bruce AGAIN?"
It's my hill. I was just trying to defend it. A good king doesn't wait for trouble to come to him, he stops it before it can get a foothold. I'm Frank the Fair, remember? This isn't just about me, it's about you two and all my friends. It's my duty to take care of you all and if that involves 'taking care' of the enemy, so be it. I absolutely won't apologise. You should be appreciative of my efforts. I'm just about tuckered out.
"Frank, if you don't stop fighting Bruce, you'll get killed. This cannot go on. Enough's enough. Now we're going to see Charlie. For heaven's sake, Frank, don't you get sick of having to see Charlie all the time?"
A bit. But I've a principle to uphold. My honour's at stake.
"Your honour's expendable, Frank E., your life isn't."

They took me to Charlie but he wasn't on duty. Instead, there was this beautiful lady vet. Her name was Rose and honestly, she was so lovely and kind and sweet and gentle and loving and everything, I could have stayed with her forever. I fell a bit in love right away and I have to say I know she felt the same. She was so gentle with me and she understood perfectly why I had to try to sort Bruce. "Poor, courageous, darling Frank," she said. "You're just being chivalrous and doing what comes naturally

aren't you dear? I'm afraid you will have to have a 'general' because you've got a big abscess and I have to fix you up."
Anything, my dear, lovely Rose, anything.
"Oh you are such a brave, wonderful cat, Frank."
And so I underwent surgery. Rose shaved my cheek and got rid of the abscess and stuck a drain in my face. I looked like a wreck but it didn't affect our feelings for each other.
"Frank E., you're a lion-heart, I have the utmost regard and respect for your dignity under extreme duress," she said as I blearily struggled to throw off the effects of the anaesthetic.
I love you, I said and fell asleep.
I stayed with Rose for two days to be sure my cheek healed. At the end of the second day Charlie came back and she had to go.
"Goodbye, Frank, dear boy."
Goodbye, my dear Rose. Perhaps we'll meet again . . . who knows?
"Nil bastardum carborundum . . . dearest."
Right, Lovely Lady! Nil bastardum indeed.
"Au Revoir."
Bye.

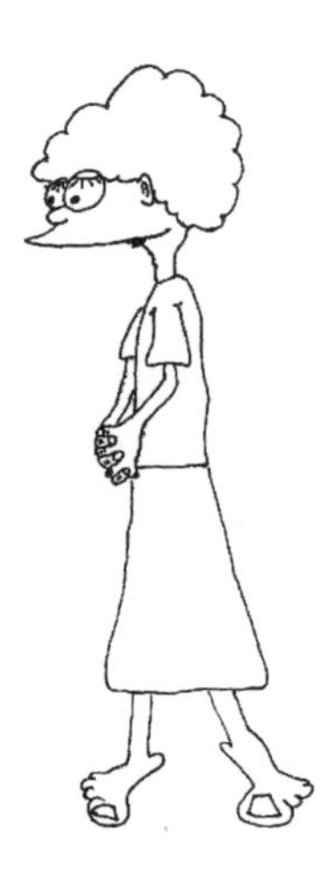

'Rough Justice' 12

Well, I was gonna need that bit of advice because you WILL NOT believe what happened when Dick and Annie came to take me home. They gave me a cuddle and asked me how I was and then just chatted to Charlie for a while about ordinary things – my health and so on. But suddenly the conversation took an ominous turn.

"He can't seem to help himself, Charlie. He's down there fighting with Bruce all the time. The irony is that it's Frank who invariably comes off worst. What're we going to do? It can't go on."

"Well," said Charlie, giggling a bit sheepishly. "We can always give him a shot of the old hormones, can't we fella?" he said, ***smiling*** at me.

I was utterly aghast, speechless with horror.

Dick and Annie exchanged conspiratorial eyebrow twitches.

"Ooh, he won't grow boobs, will he Charlie?"

Crass, dumb, stupid, ignorant woman! Embarrassment mixed with my fury.

"No, of course not, they're just androgens."

"Will he turned into a poofy-cat?"

"Hardly, he's already been 'done'."
Rough justice, rough justice!!! I screamed.
"Ssshh, Frank, don't get your knickers in a knot. What's the worst that could happen to him if he has them?" asked Dick.
"Increased appetite and more affectionate."
"It's hard to imagine him being more affectionate, he's so loving already," said Dick.
You wait, buster, you wait.
"But he's so skinny, it would be terrific if he ate more," said Annie. Well, let's give it a go."
"Right-oh," said the traitor and, before I could defend myself, in went the needle.

I waited for my trademark growl to become a squeak. I waited for my appetite to pick up. I waited to turn into a sook. Nothing happened. Odd, though. I can't be bothered going down to fight Bruce any more. I just figure the best way to beat a lout is with brains rather than brawn. Don't you reckon?

'Management Techniques' 13

I dislike the word 'manipulate'; I guess the word 'manage' would best describe my relationship with Dick and Annie. They really are quite manageable. Oh, you have to keep at them, otherwise they're liable to get a bit slack, but on the whole they're quite good. You know, once you teach humans the cues, it's just a matter of patient reminders to keep them up to scratch. For example, I'm extremely partial to being carried everywhere. So I stand up on my back legs and stretch my front legs as far up their legs as I can. Then I hook my claws into their clothes so that if they try to ignore me or move away I can just raise my back legs and swing off their clothing. They don't like it, especially if their clothing is thin because either it rips or maybe my claws dig into them a bit. So they pick me up and put me over a shoulder the way I like it and then I can steady myself by firmly inserting my claws into the nearest shoulder blade. It's a nice spot and I generally rattle very loudly into the nearest ear. They like it, I know because they smile and go sooky. I dislike being put down before I am ready. Easy enough to avoid by exerting extra claw-power.

When it comes to getting the food I want, I consider the 'aloof' method superior to all others. You ***don't*** hang around humans in the kitchen making a nuisance of yourself. All that cheap flattery, rubbing against their legs, purring and stuff, that's not going to get you the sort of cuisine you want! No, what you must do is feign indifference. When something is put in my dish, I approach it in a wide circle and with a great deal of suspicion. I inject plenty of drama into my inspection – to make sure they ***notice***. Then, I position myself as far as possible from the dish, stretch out my neck like a ferret and sniff to ascertain what's in it. If it's not what I want, I assume a look of pure repugnance, reverse backwards four or five paces, then turn my face around and stare at the offending human with a look of horrified confusion. Then I walk away as if the weight of the world is on my shoulders. YOU MUST NOT RELENT! No matter how hungry you are you must hold out for the food you want and you must repeat this process until you ***get*** the food you want. If it happens that I actually like what they put in my dish, I never appear too eager but approach the dish gingerly and nibble the contents condescendingly.

If I want some wine, it's easy. I just wait until Annie and Dick have settled down in front of telly to watch the news with a glass of red and I jump up quick and stick my face into it. That makes 'em look snappy. I have my own crystal glass. I do not drink straight from it, of course, that would be indelicate. Besides, that way they could ignore me and concentrate on the news. I am finger-fed. They have to dip their fingers in the wine over and over again so's I can lick it off. One night I got carried away and had forty-four fingers. That's pretty rare. Usually somewhere between ten and twenty is plenty for me.

All in all, they're an easy pair to manage and things are good.

I'll be five years old on the first of July. Every year we have a party but my third birthday was the best so far. Annie and Dick threw a '21st' birthday for me and we had this great big chocolate cake with a picture of me on the top. Mike and Em came and they brought me a mouse made out of mince meat with string for whiskers, currants for eyes and little shells for ears. Henry brought me a bottle of wine. Jill brought me an expensive toy which I destroyed in less than two minutes.

Life is good, don't you reckon? You wouldn't be dead for quids, would ya?

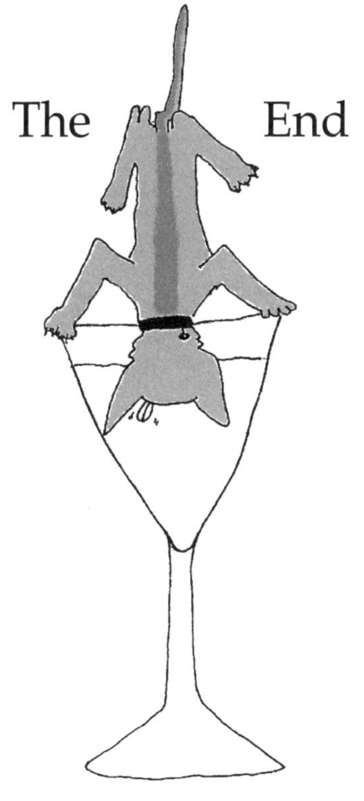